Life Lessons

from THE INSPIRED WORD of GOD

BOOK of ACTS

MAX LUCADO

General Editor

TABLE OF CONTENTS

HOW TO STUDY THE BIBLE

BY MAX LUCADO

*T*his is a peculiar book you are holding. Words crafted in another language. Deeds done in a distant era. Events recorded in a far-off land. Counsel offered to a foreign people. This is a peculiar book.

It's surprising that anyone reads it. It's too old. Some of its writings date back five thousand years. It's too bizarre. The book speaks of incredible floods, fires, earthquakes, and people with supernatural abilities. It's too radical. The Bible calls for undying devotion to a carpenter who called himself God's Son.

Logic says this book shouldn't survive. Too old, too bizarre, too radical.

The Bible has been banned, burned, scoffed, and ridiculed. Scholars have mocked it as foolish. Kings have branded it as illegal. A thousand times over it the grave has been dug and the dirge has begun, but somehow the Bible never stays in the grave. Not only has it survived, it has thrived. It is the single most popular book in all of history. It has been the best-selling book in the world for years!

There is no way on earth to explain it. Which perhaps is the only explanation. The answer? The Bible's durability is not found on earth; it is found in heaven. For the millions who have tested its claims and claimed its promises, there is but one answer—the Bible is God's book and God's voice.

As you read it, you would be wise to give some thought to two questions. What is the purpose of the Bible? and How do I study the Bible? Time spent reflecting on these two issues will greatly enhance your Bible study.

What is the purpose of the Bible?

Let the Bible itself answer that question.

Since you were a child you have known the Holy Scriptures which are able to make you wise. And that wisdom leads to salvation through faith in Christ Jesus.

(2 Tim. 3:15)

The purpose of the Bible? Salvation. God's highest passion is to get his children home. His book, the Bible, describes his plan of salvation. The purpose of the Bible is to proclaim God's plan and passion to save his children.

That is the reason this book has endured through the centuries. It dares to tackle the toughest questions about life: Where do I go after I die? Is there a God? What do I do with my fears? The Bible offers answers to these crucial questions. It is the treasure map that leads us to God's highest treasure, eternal life.

But how do we use the Bible? Countless copies of Scripture sit unread on bookshelves and nightstands simply because people don't know how to read it. What can we do to make the Bible real in our lives?

The clearest answer is found in the words of Jesus.

"Ask," he promised, *"and God will give it to you. Search and you will find. Knock, and the door will open for you."*

(Matt. 7:7)

The first step in understanding the Bible is asking God to help us. We should read prayerfully. If anyone understands God's Word, it is because of God and not the reader.

But the Helper will teach you everything and will cause you to remember all that I told you. The Helper is the Holy Spirit whom the Father will send in my name.

(John 14:24)

Before reading the Bible, pray. Invite God to speak to you. Don't go to Scripture looking for your idea, go searching for his.

Not only should we read the Bible prayerfully, we should read it carefully. *Search and you will find* is the pledge. The Bible is not a newspaper to be skimmed but rather a mine to be quarried. *Search for it like silver, and hunt for it like hidden treasure. Then you will understand respect for the LORD, and you will find that you know God* (Prov. 2:4).

Any worthy find requires effort. The Bible is no exception. To understand the Bible you don't have to be brilliant, but you must be willing to roll up your sleeves and search.

Be a worker who is not ashamed and who uses the true teaching in the right way.

(2 Tim. 2:15)

Here's a practical point. Study the Bible a bit at a time. Hunger is not satisfied by eating twenty-one meals in one sitting once a week. The body needs a steady diet to remain strong. So does the soul. When God sent food to his people in the wilderness, he didn't provide loaves already made. Instead, he sent them manna in the shape of *thin flakes, like frost . . . on the desert ground* (Exod. 16:14).

God gave manna in limited portions.

God sends spiritual food the same way. He opens the heavens with just enough nutrients for today's hunger. He provides, *a command here, a command there. A rule here, a rule there. A little lesson here, a little lesson there* (Isa. 28:10).

Don't be discouraged if your reading reaps a small harvest. Some days a lesser portion is all that is needed. What is important is to search every day for that day's message. A steady diet of God's Word over a lifetime builds a healthy soul and mind.

A little girl returned from her first day at school. Her mom asked, "Did you learn anything?" "Apparently not enough," the girl responded, "I have to go back tomorrow and the next day and the next. . . ."

Such is the case with learning. And such is the case with Bible study. Understanding comes little by little over a lifetime.

There is a third step in understanding the Bible. After the asking and seeking comes the knocking. After you ask and search, then knock.

Knock, and the door will open for you.
(Matt. 7:7)

To knock is to stand at God's door. To make yourself available. To climb the steps, cross the porch, stand at the doorway, and volunteer. Knocking goes beyond the realm of thinking and into the realm of acting.

To knock is to ask, What can I do? How can I obey? Where can I go?

It's one thing to know what to do. It's another to do it. But for those who do it, those who choose to obey, a special reward awaits them.

The truly happy are those who carefully study God's perfect law that makes people free, and they continue to study it. They do not forget what they heard, but they obey what God's teaching says. Those who do this will be made happy.
(James 1:25)

What a promise. Happiness comes to those who do what they read! It's the same with medicine. If you only read the label but ignore the pills, it won't help. It's the same with food. If you only read the recipe but never cook, you won't be fed. And it's the same with the Bible. If you only read the words but never obey, you'll never know the joy God has promised.

Ask. Search. Knock. Simple, isn't it? Why don't you give it a try? If you do, you'll see why you are holding the most remarkable book in history.

ACTS

INTRODUCTION

*T*hey aren't the same men.

Oh, I know they look like it. They have the same names. The same faces. The same mannerisms. They look the same. But they aren't. On the surface they appear no different. Peter is still brazen. Nathanael is still reflective. Philip is still calculating.

They look the same. But they aren't. They aren't the same men you read about in the last four books. The fellows you got to know in the Gospels? These are the ones, but they're different.

You'll see it. As you read you'll see it. In their eyes. You hear it in their voices. You feel it in their passion. These men have changed.

As you read you'll wonder—are these the same guys? The ones who doubted in Galilee? The ones who argued in Capernaum? The ones who ran for their lives in Gethsemane? You'll wonder, "Are these the same men?"

The answer is no. They are different. They have stood face to face with God. They have sat at the feet of the resurrected King. They are different.

Within them dwells a fire not found on earth. Christ has taught them. The Father has forgiven them. The Spirit indwells them. They are not the same.

And because they are different, so is the world.

Read their adventures and be encouraged. Read their adventures and be listening. What God did to them, he longs to do for you.

LESSON ONE

JESUS CHANGES LIVES

REFLECTION

Begin your study by sharing thoughts on this question.

1. Think of someone you love. What sacrifices have you made to make that person happy?

_____

_____

_____

BIBLE READING

Read Acts 2:36–47 from the NCV or the NKJV.

NCV

³⁶ "So, all the people of Israel should know this truly: God has made Jesus—the man you nailed to the cross—both Lord and Christ."

³⁷When the people heard this, they felt guilty and asked Peter and the other apostles, "What shall we do?"

³⁸Peter said to them, "Change your hearts and lives and be baptized, each one of you, in the name of Jesus Christ for the forgiveness of

NKJV

³⁶ "Therefore let all the house of Israel know assuredly that God has made this Jesus, whom you crucified, both Lord and Christ."

³⁷Now when they heard this, they were cut to the heart, and said to Peter and the rest of the apostles, "Men and brethren, what shall we do?"

³⁸Then Peter said to them, "Repent, and let every one of you be baptized in the name of

NCV

your sins. And you will receive the gift of the Holy Spirit. ³⁹This promise is for you, for your children, and for all who are far away. It is for everyone the Lord our God calls to himself."

⁴⁰Peter warned them with many other words. He begged them, "Save yourselves from the evil of today's people!" ⁴¹Then those people who accepted what Peter said were baptized. About three thousand people were added to the number of believers that day. ⁴²They spent their time learning the apostles' teaching, sharing, breaking bread, and praying together.

⁴³The apostles were doing many miracles and signs, and everyone felt great respect for God. ⁴⁴All the believers were together and shared everything. ⁴⁵They would sell their land and the things they owned and then divide the money and give it to anyone who needed it. ⁴⁶The believers met together in the Temple every day. They ate together in their homes, happy to share their food with joyful hearts. ⁴⁷They praised God and were liked by all the people. Every day the Lord added those who were being saved to the group of believers.

NKJV

Jesus Christ for the remission of sins; and you shall receive the gift of the Holy Spirit. ³⁹For the promise is to you and to your children, and to all who are afar off, as many as the Lord our God will call."

⁴⁰And with many other words he testified and exhorted them, saying, "Be saved from this perverse generation." ⁴¹Then those who gladly received his word were baptized; and that day about three thousand souls were added to them. ⁴²And they continued steadfastly in the apostles' doctrine and fellowship, in the breaking of bread, and in prayers. ⁴³Then fear came upon every soul, and many wonders and signs were done through the apostles. ⁴⁴Now all who believed were together, and had all things in common, ⁴⁵and sold their possessions and goods, and divided them among all, as anyone had need.

⁴⁶So continuing daily with one accord in the temple, and breaking bread from house to house, they ate their food with gladness and simplicity of heart, ⁴⁷praising God and having favor with all the people. And the Lord added to the church daily those who were being saved.

DISCOVERY

Explore the Bible reading by discussing these questions.

2. What bold statement did Peter make to the crowd?

_____

_____

_____

3. How did the people react to Peter's declaration?

_____

_____

_____

4. What instructions did Peter give to the people?

_____

_____

_____

5. To whom is the Holy Spirit available?

_____

_____

_____

6. How did the new believers grow in their faith?

_____

_____

_____

INSPIRATION

Here is an uplifting thought from the *Inspirational Study Bible.*

A transformed group stood beside a transformed Peter as he announced some weeks later: "Therefore let all Israel be assured of this: God has made this Jesus, whom you crucified, both Lord and Christ."

No timidity in his words. No reluctance. About three thousand people believed his message.

The apostles sparked a movement. The people became followers of the death-conqueror. They couldn't hear enough or say enough about him. . . . Christ was their model, their message. They preached "Jesus Christ and him crucified," not for the lack of another topic, but because they couldn't exhaust this one.

What unlocked the doors of the apostles' hearts?

Simple. They saw Jesus. They encountered the Christ. Their sins collided with their Savior and their Savior won! . . .

A lot of things would happen to them over the next few decades. Many nights would be spent away from home. Hunger would gnaw at their bellies. Rain would soak their skin. Stones would bruise their bodies. Shipwrecks, lashings, martyrdom. But there was a scene in the repertoire of memories that caused them to never look back: the betrayed coming back to find his betrayers; not to scourge them, but to send them. Not to criticize them for forgetting, but to commission them to remember. *Remember* that he who was dead is alive and they who were guilty have been forgiven.

(from *Six Hours One Friday*
by Max Lucado)

RESPONSE

Use these questions to share more deeply with each other.

7. What changes has Jesus made in your life?

_____

_____

_____

8. What circumstances caused you to open your heart to God?

_____

_____

_____

9. Why do some people resist the convicting work of the Holy Spirit?

_____

_____

_____

PRAYER

Father, we invite the powerful indwelling of your Spirit because we do not have the power to change ourselves. May we be open to your convicting work, may we be sincere, may we be willing to grow. Father, transform us into your likeness.

JOURNALING

Take a few moments to record your personal insights from this lesson.

In what area of my life have I resisted the Spirit's work?

ADDITIONAL QUESTIONS

10. The Holy Spirit gave Peter boldness to speak the truth. What ability or gift have you received from God?

_____

_____

_____

11. How have you discovered the spiritual gifts God has given you?

_____

_____

_____

12. How can you use your gifts to help bring others into God's kingdom?

_____

_____

_____

For more Bible passages about God's power to change people, see 1 Samuel 10:6; Romans 1:16, 17; 8:9–14; 16:17–19; 2 Corinthians 3:18; Galatians 5:22; Ephesians 3:16–20; Colossians 1:10–12; 28, 29; 2 Peter 1:3.

To complete the book of Acts during this twelve-part study, read Acts 1:1–2:47.

ADDITIONAL THOUGHTS

LESSON TWO

WE ARE WITNESSES

REFLECTION

Begin your study by sharing thoughts on this question.

1. Who helped you understand the truth of the gospel? How?

_____

_____

_____

BIBLE READING

Read Acts 3:1–16 from the NCV or the NKJV.

NCV

¹One day Peter and John went to the Temple at three o'clock, the time set each day for the afternoon prayer service. ²There, at the Temple gate called Beautiful Gate, was a man who had been crippled all his life. Every day he was carried to this gate to beg for money from the people going into the Temple. ³The man saw Peter and John going into the Temple and asked them for money. ⁴Peter and John looked straight at him and said, "Look at us!" ⁵The

NKJV

¹Now Peter and John went up together to the temple at the hour of prayer, the ninth hour. ²And a certain man lame from his mother's womb was carried, whom they laid daily at the gate of the temple which is called Beautiful, to ask alms from those who entered the temple; ³who, seeing Peter and John about to go into the temple, asked for alms. ⁴And fixing his eyes on him, with John, Peter said, "Look at us." ⁵So he gave them his attention, expecting to receive

NCV

man looked at them, thinking they were going to give him some money. ⁶But Peter said, "I don't have any silver or gold, but I do have something else I can give you. By the power of Jesus Christ from Nazareth, stand up and walk!" ⁷Then Peter took the man's right hand and lifted him up. Immediately the man's feet and ankles became strong. ⁸He jumped up, stood on his feet, and began to walk. He went into the Temple with them, walking and jumping and praising God. ⁹⁻¹⁰All the people recognized him as the crippled man who always sat by the Beautiful Gate begging for money. Now they saw this same man walking and praising God, and they were amazed. They wondered how this could happen.

¹¹While the man was holding on to Peter and John, all the people were amazed and ran to them at Solomon's Porch. ¹²When Peter saw this, he said to them, "People of Israel, why are you surprised? You are looking at us as if it were our own power or goodness that made this man walk. ¹³The God of Abraham, Isaac, and Jacob, the God of our ancestors, gave glory to Jesus, his servant. But you handed him over to be killed. Pilate decided to let him go free, but you told Pilate you did not want Jesus. ¹⁴You did not want the One who is holy and good but asked Pilate to give you a murderer instead. ¹⁵And so you killed the One who gives life, but God raised him from the dead. We are witnesses to this. ¹⁶It was faith in Jesus that made this crippled man well. You can see this man, and you know him. He was made completely well because of trust in Jesus, and you all saw it happen!

NKJV

something from them. ⁶Then Peter said, "Silver and gold I do not have, but what I do have I give you: In the name of Jesus Christ of Nazareth, rise up and walk." ⁷And he took him by the right hand and lifted him up, and immediately his feet and ankle bones received strength. ⁸So he, leaping up, stood and walked and entered the temple with them—walking, leaping, and praising God. ⁹And all the people saw him walking and praising God. ¹⁰Then they knew that it was he who sat begging alms at the Beautiful Gate of the temple; and they were filled with wonder and amazement at what had happened to him.

¹¹Now as the lame man who was healed held on to Peter and John, all the people ran together to them in the porch which is called Solomon's, greatly amazed. ¹²So when Peter saw it, he responded to the people: "Men of Israel, why do you marvel at this? Or why look so intently at us, as though by our own power or godliness we had made this man walk? ¹³The God of Abraham, Isaac, and Jacob, the God of our fathers, glorified His Servant Jesus, whom you delivered up and denied in the presence of Pilate, when he was determined to let Him go. ¹⁴But you denied the Holy One and the Just, and asked for a murderer to be granted to you, ¹⁵and killed the Prince of life, whom God raised from the dead, of which we are witnesses. ¹⁶And His name, through faith in His name, has made this man strong, whom you see and know. Yes, the faith which comes through Him has given him this perfect soundness in the presence of you all.

DISCOVERY

Explore the Bible reading by discussing these questions.

2. What were Peter and John unable to give the crippled man? What did they give?

_____

_____

_____

3. How did the crippled man react to the miracle?

_____

_____

_____

4. How did the people at the temple respond to Peter and John after they heard about the miracle?

_____

_____

_____

5. What opportunity did this miracle provide for Peter?

_____

_____

_____

6. How did Peter explain the healing of the crippled man?

_____

_____

_____

INSPIRATION

Here is an uplifting thought from the *Inspirational Study Bible.*

Most believers are convinced that it is the pastor's responsibility to bring people into the church as well as into the kingdom of God. Nothing could be further from the truth. The Scripture is clear on this point. Pastors were given by God to the church to equip the people to do the work. . . . Sermons are not God's primary method for reaching people. People are His method for reaching people. What kind of people? Men and women whose lives and life-styles have been deeply affected by the truths of Scripture, people who have discovered the wonderful Spirit-filled life.

God is looking for imperfect men and women who have learned to walk in moment-by-moment dependence on the Holy Spirit. Christians who have come to terms with their inadequacies, fears, and failures. Believers who have become discontent with "surviving" and have taken the time to investigate everything God has to offer in this life.

God's method for reaching this generation, and every generation, is not preachers and sermons. It is Christians whose life-styles are empowered and directed by the Holy Spirit. People are the key to reaching people!

(from *The Wonderful Spirit-Filled Life* by Charles Stanley)

RESPONSE

Use these questions to share more deeply with each other.

7. What can we learn from Peter's example about spreading the gospel?

_____

_____

_____

8. Why is it important for us to encourage others to follow Jesus?

_____

_____

_____

9. What does it mean to be bold witnesses for Christ?

_____

_____

_____

PRAYER

Father, you give us many opportunities to proclaim your salvation message, yet we often shirk back from those opportunities in fearful silence. Forgive us, Father. Fill us with courage to boldly speak the truth in love. Teach us what it means to be your witnesses.

JOURNALING

Take a few moments to record your personal insights from this lesson.

How have I used the opportunities God has given me to share the gospel?

ADDITIONAL QUESTIONS

10. What excuses do Christians use to keep quiet about their faith?

_____

_____

_____

11. What steps can you take to prepare yourself to explain the gospel to others?

_____

_____

_____

12. Think of one person who does not know Christ. When can you share the gospel with that person?

_____

_____

_____

For more Bible passages about witnessing, see Mark 5:19; 16:15; Acts 1:8; 2 Corinthians 4:13, 14; Colossians 4:5, 6; 2 Timothy 4:2; 1 Peter 3:15, 16.

To complete the book of Acts during this twelve-part study, read Acts 3:1–4:37.

ADDITIONAL THOUGHTS

LESSON THREE

TRIED AND TESTED

REFLECTION

Begin your study by sharing thoughts on this question.

1. Think of someone who has boldly stood up for what is right. What made that person's stance so courageous?

_____

_____

_____

BIBLE READING

Read Acts 5:17–33 from the NCV or the NKJV.

NCV

¹⁷The high priest and all his friends (a group called the Sadducees) became very jealous. ¹⁸They took the apostles and put them in jail. ¹⁹But during the night, an angel of the Lord opened the doors of the jail and led the apostles outside. The angel said, ²⁰"Go stand in the Temple and tell the people everything about

NKJV

¹⁷Then the high priest rose up, and all those who were with him (which is the sect of the Sadducees), and they were filled with indignation, ¹⁸and laid their hands on the apostles and put them in the common prison. ¹⁹But at night an angel of the Lord opened the prison doors and brought them out, and said, ²⁰ "Go, stand

NCV

this new life." [21]When the apostles heard this, they obeyed and went into the Temple early in the morning and continued teaching.

When the high priest and his friends arrived, they called a meeting of the Jewish leaders and all the important older Jewish men. They sent some men to the jail to bring the apostles to them. [22]But, upon arriving, the officers could not find the apostles. So they went back and reported to the Jewish leaders. [23]They said, "The jail was closed and locked, and the guards were standing at the doors. But when we opened the doors, the jail was empty!" [24]Hearing this, the captain of the Temple guards and the leading priests were confused and wondered what was happening.

[25]Then someone came and told them, "Listen! The men you put in jail are standing in the Temple teaching the people." [26]Then the captain and his men went out and brought the apostles back. But the soldiers did not use force, because they were afraid the people would stone them to death.

[27]The soldiers brought the apostles to the meeting and made them stand before the Jewish leaders. The high priest questioned them, [28]saying, "We gave you strict orders not to continue teaching in that name. But look, you have filled Jerusalem with your teaching and are trying to make us responsible for this man's death."

[29]Peter and the other apostles answered, "We must obey God, not human authority! [30]You killed Jesus by hanging him on a cross. But God, the God of our ancestors, raised Jesus up from the dead! [31]Jesus is the One whom God

NKJV

in the temple and speak to the people all the words of this life."

[21]And when they heard that, they entered the temple early in the morning and taught. But the high priest and those with him came and called the council together, with all the elders of the children of Israel, and sent to the prison to have them brought.

[22]But when the officers came and did not find them in the prison, they returned and reported, [23]saying, "Indeed we found the prison shut securely, and the guards standing outside before the doors; but when we opened them, we found no one inside!" [24]Now when the high priest, the captain of the temple, and the chief priests heard these things, they wondered what the outcome would be. [25]So one came and told them, saying, "Look, the men whom you put in prison are standing in the temple and teaching the people!"

[26]Then the captain went with the officers and brought them without violence, for they feared the people, lest they should be stoned. [27]And when they had brought them, they set them before the council. And the high priest asked them, [28]saying, "Did we not strictly command you not to teach in this name? And look, you have filled Jerusalem with your doctrine, and intend to bring this Man's blood on us!"

[29]But Peter and the other apostles answered and said: "We ought to obey God rather than men. [30]The God of our fathers raised up Jesus whom you murdered by hanging on a tree. [31]Him God has exalted to His right hand to be Prince and Savior, to give repentance to Israel

NCV

raised to be on his right side, as Leader and Savior. Through him, all Jewish people could change their hearts and lives and have their sins forgiven. ³²We saw all these things happen. The Holy Spirit, whom God has given to all who obey him, also proves these things are true."

³³When the Jewish leaders heard this, they became angry and wanted to kill them.

NKJV

and forgiveness of sins. ³²And we are His witnesses to these things, and so also is the Holy Spirit whom God has given to those who obey Him."

³³When they heard this, they were furious and plotted to kill them.

DISCOVERY

Explore the Bible reading by discussing these questions.

2. What was the problem between the apostles and the religious leaders?

_____

_____

_____

3. How did the high priest try to stop the disciples from preaching?

_____

_____

_____

4. How were the disciples able to continue their ministry?

_____

_____

_____

5. What accusations did the high priest make against Peter and the other apostles?

_____

_____

_____

6. How did the apostles deal with the opposition of the religious leaders?

_____

_____

_____

INSPIRATION

Here is an uplifting thought from the *Inspirational Study Bible.*

On God's anvil. Perhaps you've been there.

Melted down. Formless. Undone.

I know. I've been on it. It's rough. It's a spiritual slump, a famine. The fire goes out. Although the fire may flame for a moment, it soon disappears. We drift downward. Downward into the foggy valley of question, the misty lowland of discouragement. Motivation wanes. Desire is distant. Responsibilities are depressing.

Passion? It slips out the door.

Enthusiasm? Are you kidding?

Anvil time.

It can be caused by a death, a breakup, going broke, going prayerless. The light switch is flipped off and the room darkens. "All the thoughtful words of help and hope have all been nicely said. But I'm still hurting, wondering. . . ."

On the anvil.

Brought face to face with God out of the utter realization that we have nowhere else to go. Jesus, in the garden. Peter, with a tear-streamed face. David, after Bathsheba. Elijah and the "still, small voice." Paul, blind in Damascus.

Pound, pound, pound.

I hope you're not on the anvil. (Unless you need to be and, if so, I hope you are.) Anvil time is not to be avoided; it's to be experienced. Although the tunnel is dark, it does go through the mountain. Anvil time reminds us of who we are and who God is. We shouldn't try to escape it. To escape it could be to escape God.

God sees our life from beginning to end. He may lead us through a storm at age thirty so we can endure a hurricane at age sixty. An instrument is useful only if it's in the right shape. A dull ax or a bent screwdriver needs attention, and so do we. A good blacksmith keeps his tools in shape. So does God.

Should God place you on his anvil, be thankful. It means he thinks you're still worth reshaping.

(from *On the Anvil*
by Max Lucado)

RESPONSE

Use these questions to share more deeply with each other.

7. What do people usually do when life gets difficult?

_____

_____

_____

8. What lessons can be learned from experiencing pain?

_____

_____

_____

9. What good has come from a difficult experience in your life?

_____

_____

_____

PRAYER

Father, we believe that when we meet you face-to-face, any trials that we endured on this earth will seem small. Help us remember that any earthly struggle is small in comparison to the great God we serve.

JOURNALING

Take a few moments to record your personal insights from this lesson.

How do I need to change my attitudes toward problems and difficulties in my life?

ADDITIONAL QUESTIONS

10. What opposition do believers face today?

_____

_____

_____

11. What can we learn from the apostles' example about coping with criticism and unfair treatment?

_____

_____

_____

12. How can we develop a joyful spirit?

_____

_____

_____

For more Bible passages about trials and testing, see Genesis 22:1; Job 23:10; Psalm 66:10; Isaiah 48:10; 2 Corinthians 4:8, 9, 16–18; 2 Thessalonians 1:4–7; Hebrews 10:32–34; James 1:2–4, 12; 5:10, 11; 1 Peter 2:20, 21; 4:12–19; 5:10.

To complete the book of Acts during this twelve-part study, read Acts 5:1–42.

LESSON FOUR

GETTING ALONG WITH OTHERS

REFLECTION

Begin your study by sharing thoughts on this question.

1. What is the best advice you've heard about getting along with people? How have you put it into practice?

_____

_____

_____

BIBLE READING

Read Acts 6:1–15 from the NCV or the NKJV.

NCV

¹The number of followers was growing. But during this same time, the Greek-speaking followers had an argument with the other Jewish followers. The Greek-speaking widows were not getting their share of the food that was given out every day. ²The twelve apostles called the whole group of followers together and said,

NKJV

¹Now in those days, when the number of the disciples was multiplying, there arose a complaint against the Hebrews by the Hellenists, because their widows were neglected in the daily distribution. ²Then the twelve summoned the multitude of the disciples and said, "It is not desirable that we should leave the word of God

NCV

"It is not right for us to stop our work of teaching God's word in order to serve tables. ³So, brothers and sisters, choose seven of your own men who are good, full of the Spirit and full of wisdom. We will put them in charge of this work. ⁴Then we can continue to pray and to teach the word of God."

⁵The whole group liked the idea, so they chose these seven men: Stephen (a man with great faith and full of the Holy Spirit), Philip, Procorus, Nicanor, Timon, Parmenas, and Nicolas (a man from Antioch who had become a Jew). ⁶Then they put these men before the apostles, who prayed and laid their hands on them.

⁷The word of God was continuing to spread. The group of followers in Jerusalem increased, and a great number of the Jewish priests believed and obeyed.

⁸Stephen was richly blessed by God who gave him the power to do great miracles and signs among the people. ⁹But some Jewish people were against him. They belonged to the synagogue of Free Men (as it was called), which included Jewish people from Cyrene, Alexandria, Cilicia, and Asia. They all came and argued with Stephen.

¹⁰But the Spirit was helping him to speak with wisdom, and his words were so strong that they could not argue with him. ¹¹So they secretly urged some men to say, "We heard Stephen speak against Moses and against God."

¹²This upset the people, the older Jewish leaders, and the teachers of the law. They came and grabbed Stephen and brought him to a meeting of the Jewish leaders. ¹³They brought

NKJV

and serve tables. ³Therefore, brethren, seek out from among you seven men of good reputation, full of the Holy Spirit and wisdom, whom we may appoint over this business; ⁴but we will give ourselves continually to prayer and to the ministry of the word."

⁵And the saying pleased the whole multitude. And they chose Stephen, a man full of faith and the Holy Spirit, and Philip, Prochorus, Nicanor, Timon, Parmenas, and Nicolas, a proselyte from Antioch, ⁶whom they set before the apostles; and when they had prayed, they laid hands on them.

⁷Then the word of God spread, and the number of the disciples multiplied greatly in Jerusalem, and a great many of the priests were obedient to the faith.

⁸And Stephen, full of faith and power, did great wonders and signs among the people. ⁹Then there arose some from what is called the Synagogue of the Freedmen (Cyrenians, Alexandrians, and those from Cilicia and Asia), disputing with Stephen. ¹⁰And they were not able to resist the wisdom and the Spirit by which he spoke. ¹¹Then they secretly induced men to say, "We have heard him speak blasphemous words against Moses and God." ¹²And they stirred up the people, the elders, and the scribes; and they came upon him, seized him, and brought him to the council. ¹³They also set up false witnesses who said, "This man does not cease to speak blasphemous words against this holy place and the law; ¹⁴for we have heard him say that this Jesus of Nazareth will destroy this place and change the customs which Moses delivered to us." ¹⁵And all who sat in the

NCV

in some people to tell lies about Stephen, saying, "This man is always speaking against this holy place and the law of Moses. [14]We heard him say that Jesus from Nazareth will destroy this place and that Jesus will change the customs Moses gave us." [15]All the people in the meeting were watching Stephen closely and saw that his face looked like the face of an angel.

NKJV

council, looking steadfastly at him, saw his face as the face of an angel.

DISCOVERY

Explore the Bible reading by discussing these questions.

2. What problem arose in the early church?

_____

_____

_____

3. What solution did the apostles offer?

_____

_____

_____

4. How did the group respond to the apostles' idea?

_____

_____

_____

5. What does this passage reveal about Stephen's character and relationship with God?

_____

_____

_____

6. How did God use Stephen to help the early church?

_____

_____

_____

INSPIRATION

Here is an uplifting thought from the *Inspirational Study Bible.*

Who are the people you know who appear to get along well with others? What is so special about them? What qualities do they possess which make them people persons? The people I know who get along well with others are enjoyable to be with. They show genuine interest in others. When they are with you, they are really with you.

I think of a man I know who is very gracious, friendly, and refined in his dealings with people, whether they are his friends, his co-workers, or the waiters who serve him. His pleasant manner is not put on; it's genuine. And he gets along with almost everybody. When I'm with him, he treats me as an individual. I am accepted for who I am and viewed by him as a person of worth. He listens to me and appreci-ates my contributions to the conversation.

A man who encourages and builds up others, he is compassionate and empathetic, touching people in times of joy and sorrow. He fits the description of a likable character I read about recently in a novel. This man was described as "large-hearted with everyone." The way my friend treats the people in his life is how most people want to be treated.

Do these qualities describe how you would like to be treated? Are these qualities evident in your dealings with others? It takes time to develop the qualities I find in my friend. I'm still working on them in my life. Fortunately, we all have the capacity to learn them and put them into practice.

(from *How to Get Along with Almost Anyone* by H. Norman Wright)

RESPONSE

Use these questions to share more deeply with each other.

7. What causes tension and disagreements in the church today?

_____

_____

_____

8. Why is it important for Christians to get along?

_____

_____

_____

9. What can we learn from the early church leaders about resolving our differences?

_____

_____

_____

PRAYER

Father, we pray that your church would be unified in love and purpose. Teach us how to sow seeds of peace and harmony. Help us to resolve our differences lovingly, so that unbelievers would be drawn into your family because of the love we share.

JOURNALING

Take a few moments to record your personal insights from this lesson.

What do I usually do when I feel tension in a relationship? How can I improve the way I resolve conflicts?

ADDITIONAL QUESTIONS

10. What happens when believers criticize and argue with one another?

_____

_____

_____

11. What character traits do believers need to get along with each other?

_____

_____

_____

12. How can we cultivate these qualities?

_____

_____

_____

For more Bible passages about getting along with people, see Proverbs 17:14; Romans 12:16; 15:5–7; 1 Corinthians 1:10; 3:3; 6:1–7; Ephesians 4:2–4; Philippians 2:3, 4; 1 Thessalonians 5:12–15; Hebrews 12:14; 1 Peter 3:8, 9.

To complete the book of Acts during this twelve-part study, read Acts 6:1–15.

ADDITIONAL THOUGHTS

LESSON FIVE

LOOKING TO JESUS

REFLECTION

Begin your study by sharing thoughts on this question.

1. If you were on your deathbed, what would you want to say to your family and friends? Why?

_____

_____

_____

BIBLE READING

Read Acts 7:51–60 from the NCV or the NKJV.

NCV

⁵¹Stephen continued speaking: "You stubborn people! You have not given your hearts to God, nor will you listen to him! You are always against what the Holy Spirit is trying to tell you, just as your ancestors were. ⁵²Your ancestors tried to hurt every prophet who ever lived. Those prophets said long ago that the One who is good would come, but your ancestors killed them. And now you have turned against and

NKJV

⁵¹"You stiffnecked and uncircumcised in heart and ears! You always resist the Holy Spirit; as your fathers did, so do you. ⁵²Which of the prophets did your fathers not persecute? And they killed those who foretold the coming of the Just One, of whom you now have become the betrayers and murderers, ⁵³who have received the law by the direction of angels and have not kept it."

killed the One who is good. ⁵³You received the law of Moses, which God gave you through his angels, but you haven't obeyed it."

⁵⁴When the leaders heard this, they became furious. They were so mad they were grinding their teeth at Stephen. ⁵⁵But Stephen was full of the Holy Spirit. He looked up to heaven and saw the glory of God and Jesus standing at God's right side. ⁵⁶He said, "Look! I see heaven open and the Son of Man standing at God's right side."

⁵⁷Then they shouted loudly and covered their ears and all ran at Stephen. ⁵⁸They took him out of the city and began to throw stones at him to kill him. And those who told lies against Stephen left their coats with a young man named Saul. ⁵⁹While they were throwing stones, Stephen prayed, "Lord Jesus, receive my spirit." ⁶⁰He fell on his knees and cried in a loud voice, "Lord, do not hold this sin against them." After Stephen said this, he died.

⁵⁴When they heard these things they were cut to the heart, and they gnashed at him with their teeth. ⁵⁵But he, being full of the Holy Spirit, gazed into heaven and saw the glory of God, and Jesus standing at the right hand of God, ⁵⁶and said, "Look! I see the heavens opened and the Son of Man standing at the right hand of God!"

⁵⁷Then they cried out with a loud voice, stopped their ears, and ran at him with one accord; ⁵⁸and they cast him out of the city and stoned him. And the witnesses laid down their clothes at the feet of a young man named Saul. ⁵⁹And they stoned Stephen as he was calling on God and saying, "Lord Jesus, receive my spirit." ⁶⁰Then he knelt down and cried out with a loud voice, "Lord, do not charge them with this sin." And when he had said this, he fell asleep.

DISCOVERY

Explore the Bible reading by discussing these questions.

2. What accusations did Stephen make against the members of the ruling council?

_____

_____

_____

3. To whom did Stephen compare the religious leaders? Why?

_____

_____

_____

4. Why did Stephen's speech infuriate his adversaries?

_____

_____

_____

5. How did Stephen face his impending death?

_____

_____

_____

6. What do Stephen's last words reveal about his character?

_____

_____

_____

INSPIRATION

Here is an uplifting thought from the *Inspirational Study Bible*.

The story of young Matthew Huffman came across my desk the week I was writing this chapter. He was the six-year-old son of missionaries in Salvador, Brazil. One morning he began to complain of fever. As his temperature went up, he began losing his eyesight. His mother and father put him in the car and raced him to the hospital.

As they were driving and he was lying on his mother's lap, he did something his parents will never forget. He extended his hand in the air. His mother took it and he pulled it away. He extended it again. She again took it and he, again, pulled it back and reached into the air.

Confused, the mother asked her son, "What are you reaching for, Matthew?"

"I'm reaching for Jesus' hand," he answered. And with those words he closed his eyes and slid into a coma from which he never would awaken. He died two days later, a victim of bacterial meningitis.

Of all the things he didn't learn in his short life, he'd learned the most important: who to reach for in the hour of death.

(from *And the Angels Were Silent*
by Max Lucado)

RESPONSE

Use these questions to share more deeply with each other.

7. Why do you think Stephen was able to face death courageously?

_____

_____

_____

8. How does Stephen's example encourage you?

_____

_____

_____

9. Why do you suppose we look to ourselves for strength rather than depend on God?

_____

_____

_____

PRAYER

Father, put your hands and your arms around us and embrace us. Carry us through the valleys, giving us strength for today and courage for tomorrow. Teach us to seek you in all things. May we seek you forever.

JOURNALING

Take a few moments to record your personal insights from this lesson.

In what area of my life do I need Jesus' help? How can I show my dependence on him?

ADDITIONAL QUESTIONS

10. Where do you usually turn for help when you are in trouble?

_____

_____

_____

11. What happens when we depend on ourselves or others to carry us through painful experiences?

_____

_____

_____

12. Think of an instance when you- received God's help during a difficult time. What happened?

_____

_____

_____

For more Bible passages about turning to God, see Psalm 34:5; 105:4; 142:5, 6; Acts 3:19; Hebrews 3:1; 12:2; 1 Peter 5:9.

To complete the book of Acts during this twelve-part study, read Acts 7:1–60.

ADDITIONAL THOUGHTS

LESSON SIX

THE HOLY SPIRIT'S LEADING

REFLECTION

Begin your study by sharing thoughts on this question.

1. Think of a time when you felt compelled to help someone? What did you do to help that person?

_____

_____

_____

BIBLE READING

Read Acts 8:26–40 from the NCV or the NKJV.

NCV

²⁶An angel of the Lord said to Philip, "Get ready and go south to the road that leads down to Gaza from Jerusalem—the desert road." ²⁷So Philip got ready and went. On the road he saw a man from Ethiopia, a eunuch. He was an important officer in the service of Candace, the queen of the Ethiopians; he was responsible for taking care of all her money. He had gone to Jerusalem to worship. ²⁸Now, as he was on his

NKJV

²⁶Now an angel of the Lord spoke to Philip, saying, "Arise and go toward the south along the road which goes down from Jerusalem to Gaza." This is desert. ²⁷So he arose and went. And behold, a man of Ethiopia, a eunuch of great authority under Candace the queen of the Ethiopians, who had charge of all her treasury, and had come to Jerusalem to worship, ²⁸was returning. And sitting in his chariot, he was

way home, he was sitting in his chariot reading from the Book of Isaiah, the prophet. [29]The Spirit said to Philip, "Go to that chariot and stay near it."

[30]So when Philip ran toward the chariot, he heard the man reading from Isaiah the prophet. Philip asked, "Do you understand what you are reading?"

[31]He answered, "How can I understand unless someone explains it to me?" Then he invited Philip to climb in and sit with him. [32]The portion of Scripture he was reading was this:

"He was like a sheep being led to be killed.
  He was quiet, as a lamb is quiet while its
    wool is being cut;
  he never opened his mouth.
[33]He was shamed and was treated unfairly.
He died without children to continue his
    family.
  His life on earth has ended."

[34]The officer said to Philip, "Please tell me, who is the prophet talking about—himself or someone else?" [35]Philip began to speak, and starting with this same Scripture, he told the man the Good News about Jesus.

[36]While they were traveling down the road, they came to some water. The officer said, "Look, here is water. What is stopping me from being baptized?" [38]Then the officer commanded the chariot to stop. Both Philip and the officer went down into the water, and Philip baptized him. [39]When they came up out of the water, the Spirit of the Lord took Philip away; the officer never saw him again. And the officer continued on his way home, full of joy. [40]But

reading Isaiah the prophet. [29]Then the Spirit said to Philip, "Go near and overtake this chariot."

[30]So Philip ran to him, and heard him reading the prophet Isaiah, and said, "Do you understand what you are reading?"

[31]And he said, "How can I, unless someone guides me?" And he asked Philip to come up and sit with him. [32]The place in the Scripture which he read was this:

"He was led as a sheep to the slaughter;
And as a lamb before its shearer is silent,
So He opened not His mouth.
[33]In His humiliation His justice was taken
    away,
And who will declare His generation?
For His life is taken from the earth."

[34]So the eunuch answered Philip and said, "I ask you, of whom does the prophet say this, of himself or of some other man?" [35]Then Philip opened his mouth, and beginning at this Scripture, preached Jesus to him. [36]Now as they went down the road, they came to some water. And the eunuch said, "See, here is water. What hinders me from being baptized?"

[37]Then Philip said, "If you believe with all your heart, you may."

And he answered and said, "I believe that Jesus Christ is the Son of God."

[38]So he commanded the chariot to stand still. And both Philip and the eunuch went down into the water, and he baptized him. [39]Now when they came up out of the water, the Spirit of the Lord caught Philip away, so that the

NCV

Philip appeared in a city called Azotus and preached the Good News in all the towns on the way from Azotus to Caesarea.

NKJV

eunuch saw him no more; and he went on his way rejoicing. [40]But Philip was found at Azotus. And passing through, he preached in all the cities till he came to Caesarea.

DISCOVERY

Explore the Bible reading by discussing these questions.

2. What examples of the Holy Spirit's leading do you see in this story?

_____

_____

_____

3. Why did God ask Philip to leave his preaching and go down a desert road?

_____

_____

_____

4. What was significant about the person Philip encountered on the road?

_____

_____

_____

5. How did Philip handle the opportunity that God gave him?

_____

_____

_____

6. What was the result of Philip's obedience to God?

_____

_____

_____

INSPIRATION

Here is an uplifting thought from the *Inspirational Study Bible.*
You've heard the voice whispering your name, haven't you? You've felt the nudge to go and sensed

the urge to speak. Hasn't it occurred to you?

You invite a couple over for coffee. Nothing heroic, just a nice evening with old friends. But from the moment you enter, you can feel the tension. Colder than glaciers, they are. You can tell something is wrong. Typically you're not one to inquire, but you feel a concern that won't be silent. So you ask.

You are in a business meeting where one of your co-workers gets raked over the coals. Everyone else is thinking, *I'm glad that wasn't me.* But the Holy Spirit is leading you to think, *How hard this must be.* So, after the meeting you approach the employee and express your concern.

You notice the fellow on the other side of the church auditorium. He looks a bit out of place, what with his strange clothing and all. You learn that he is from Africa, in town on business. The next Sunday he is back. And the third Sunday he is present. You introduce yourself. He tells you how he is fascinated by the faith and how he wants to learn more. Rather than offer to teach him, you simply urge him to read the Bible.

Later in the week, you regret not being more direct. You call the office where he is consulting and learn that he is leaving today for home. You know in your heart you can't let him leave. So you rush to the airport and find him awaiting his flight, with a Bible open on his lap.

"Do you understand what you are reading?" you inquire.

"How can I, unless someone explains it to me?"

And so you, like Philip, explain. And he, like the Ethiopian, believes. Baptism is requested and baptism is offered. He catches a later flight and you catch a glimpse of what it means to be led by the Spirit.

Were there lights? You just lit one. Were there voices? You just were one. Was there a miracle? You just witnessed one. Who knows? If the Bible were being written today, that might be your name in the eighth chapter of Acts.

(from *When God Whispers Your Name*
by Max Lucado)

RESPONSE

Use these questions to share more deeply with each other.

7. How does God's Spirit lead us?

_____

_____

_____

8. Why is it important to be sensitive to the Holy Spirit?

_____

_____

_____

9. How can we learn to recognize God's voice?

_____

_____

_____

PRAYER

Father, too many times we fail to hear you speaking to us. Remind us to be quiet before you so that we can hear your voice. May we make decisions based on your leading, not according to our goals and desires. But most of all, Father, help us to cherish the gift of your Spirit.

JOURNALING

Take a few moments to record your personal insights from this lesson.

What can I do to listen to the Spirit's guidance today?

ADDITIONAL QUESTIONS

10. When have you felt the Holy Spirit nudging you? What did you do?

_____

_____

_____

11. What holds us back from obeying God?

_____

_____

_____

12. What is the potential danger in ignoring the Spirit's leading?

_____

_____

_____

For more Bible passages about the Holy Spirit's leading, see Matthew 4:1; Luke 4:18; John 6:63; 14:26; 16:13; Acts 2:4; Romans 8:5, 26, 27; Galatians 5:25; 2 Peter 1:21.

To complete the book of Acts during this twelve-part study, read Acts 8:1–40.

LESSON SEVEN

GOD'S SAVING POWER

REFLECTION

Begin your study by sharing thoughts on this question.

1. Think of a time you have seen God's power revealed in the life of a friend. What happened to that person?

_____

_____

_____

BIBLE READING

Read Acts 9:3–20 from the NCV or the NKJV.

NCV

³So Saul headed toward Damascus. As he came near the city, a bright light from heaven suddenly flashed around him. ⁴Saul fell to the ground and heard a voice saying to him, "Saul, Saul! Why are you persecuting me?"

⁵Saul said, "Who are you, Lord?"

The voice answered, "I am Jesus, whom you

NKJV

³As he journeyed he came near Damascus, and suddenly a light shone around him from heaven. ⁴Then he fell to the ground, and heard a voice saying to him, "Saul, Saul, why are you persecuting Me?"

⁵And he said, "Who are You, Lord?"

Then the Lord said, "I am Jesus, whom

are persecuting. ⁶Get up now and go into the city. Someone there will tell you what you must do."

⁷The people traveling with Saul stood there but said nothing. They heard the voice, but they saw no one. ⁸Saul got up from the ground and opened his eyes, but he could not see. So those with Saul took his hand and led him into Damascus. ⁹For three days Saul could not see and did not eat or drink.

¹⁰There was a follower of Jesus in Damascus named Ananias. The Lord spoke to Ananias in a vision, "Ananias!"

Ananias answered, "Here I am, Lord."

¹¹The Lord said to him, "Get up and go to Straight Street. Find the house of Judas, and ask for a man named Saul from the city of Tarsus. He is there now, praying. ¹²Saul has seen a vision in which a man named Ananias comes to him and lays his hands on him. Then he is able to see again."

¹³But Ananias answered, "Lord, many people have told me about this man and the terrible things he did to your holy people in Jerusalem. ¹⁴Now he has come here to Damascus, and the leading priests have given him the power to arrest everyone who worships you."

¹⁵But the Lord said to Ananias, "Go! I have chosen Saul for an important work. He must tell about me to those who are not Jews, to kings, and to the people of Israel. ¹⁶I will show him how much he must suffer for my name."

¹⁷So Ananias went to the house of Judas. He laid his hands on Saul and said, "Brother Saul, the Lord Jesus sent me. He is the one you saw on the road on your way here. He sent me so

you are persecuting. It is hard for you to kick against the goads."

⁶So he, trembling and astonished, said, "Lord, what do You want me to do?"

Then the Lord said to him, "Arise and go into the city, and you will be told what you must do."

⁷And the men who journeyed with him stood speechless, hearing a voice but seeing no one. ⁸Then Saul arose from the ground, and when his eyes were opened he saw no one. But they led him by the hand and brought him into Damascus. ⁹And he was three days without sight, and neither ate nor drank.

¹⁰Now there was a certain disciple at Damascus named Ananias; and to him the Lord said in a vision, "Ananias."

And he said, "Here I am, Lord."

¹¹So the Lord said to him, "Arise and go to the street called Straight, and inquire at the house of Judas for one called Saul of Tarsus, for behold, he is praying. ¹²And in a vision he has seen a man named Ananias coming in and putting his hand on him, so that he might receive his sight."

¹³Then Ananias answered, "Lord, I have heard from many about this man, how much harm he has done to Your saints in Jerusalem. ¹⁴And here he has authority from the chief priests to bind all who call on Your name."

¹⁵But the Lord said to him, "Go, for he is a chosen vessel of Mine to bear My name before Gentiles, kings, and the children of Israel. ¹⁶For I will show him how many things he must suffer for My name's sake."

¹⁷And Ananias went his way and entered the

NCV

that you can see again and be filled with the Holy Spirit." [18]Immediately, something that looked like fish scales fell from Saul's eyes, and he was able to see again! Then Saul got up and was baptized. [19]After he ate some food, his strength returned.

Saul stayed with the followers of Jesus in Damascus for a few days. [20]Soon he began to preach about Jesus in the synagogues, saying, "Jesus is the Son of God."

NKJV

house; and laying his hands on him he said, "Brother Saul, the Lord Jesus, who appeared to you on the road as you came, has sent me that you may receive your sight and be filled with the Holy Spirit." [18]Immediately there fell from his eyes something like scales, and he received his sight at once; and he arose and was baptized.

[19]So when he had received food, he was strengthened. Then Saul spent some days with the disciples at Damascus.

[20]Immediately he preached the Christ in the synagogues, that He is the Son of God.

DISCOVERY

Explore the Bible reading by discussing these questions.

2. Whom did Saul meet on his way to Damascus? How?

_____

_____

_____

3. What did the voice from heaven tell Saul about his past and his future?

_____

_____

_____

4. How long did Saul have to wait for further instructions from the Lord?

_____

_____

_____

5. How did Ananias minister to Saul?

_____

_____

_____

6. How was God's power revealed in Saul's life?

_____

_____

_____

INSPIRATION

Here is an uplifting thought from the *Inspirational Study Bible.*

Before he encountered Christ, Paul had been somewhat of a hero among the Pharisees. . . .

Blue-blooded and wild-eyed, this young zealot was hellbent on keeping the kingdom pure—and that meant keeping the Christians out. He marched through the countryside like a general demanding that backslidden Jews salute the flag of the motherland or kiss their family and hopes good-bye.

All this came to a halt, however, on the shoulder of a highway. . . . That's when someone slammed on the stadium slights, and he heard the voice.

When he found out whose voice it was, his jaw hit the ground, and his body followed. He braced himself for the worst. He knew it was all over. . . . He prayed that death would be quick and painless.

But all he got was silence and the first of a lifetime of surprises.

He ended up bewildered and befuddled in a borrowed bedroom. God left him there a few days with scales on his eyes so thick that the only direction he could look was inside himself. And he didn't like what he saw.

He saw himself for what he really was—to use his own words, the worst of sinners.

. . . Alone in the room with his sins on his conscience and blood on his hands, he asked to be cleansed.

. . . The legalist Saul was buried, and the liberator Paul was born. He was never the same afterwards. And neither was the world. . . .

The message is gripping: Show a man his failures without Jesus, and the result will be found in the roadside gutter. Give a man religion without reminding him of his filth, and the result will be arrogance in a three-piece suit. But get the two in the same heart—get sin to meet Savior and Savior to meet sin—and the result just might be another Pharisee turned preacher who sets the world on fire.

(from *The Applause of Heaven*
by Max Lucado)

RESPONSE

Use these questions to share more deeply with each other.

7. With which person in the story do you identify: Saul, his companions, or Ananias? Explain.

_____

_____

_____

8. What does this passage teach us about God? About people?

_____

_____

_____

9. Describe your conversion experience. Why is it helpful to share our stories with one another?

_____

_____

_____

PRAYER

Father, when we think of what you have done for us, we feel only humble gratitude. We can never thank you enough for sacrificing your Son to save us. You rescued us from an eternity of suffering and offered us everlasting joy. We praise you, Father, for displaying your saving power in us.

JOURNALING

Take a few moments to record your personal insights from this lesson.

How can I thank God for saving me?

ADDITIONAL QUESTIONS

10. List some of the ways God can use us to minister to unbelievers.

_____

_____

_____

11. Think of a time when God used you to minister to someone else. What did you do?

_____

_____

_____

12. How can you minister to someone who has not yet experienced God's saving power?

_____

_____

_____

For more Bible passages about God's power to save, see Psalm 68:20; Daniel 3:17; Zephaniah 3:17; Matthew 1:21; John 3:3–8, 16–21; 6:44, 65; Acts 22:14–16; Romans 10:9–13; Hebrews 7:25.

To complete the book of Acts during this twelve-part study, read Acts 9:1–43.

LESSON EIGHT

UNITY AMONG BELIEVERS

REFLECTION

Begin your study by sharing thoughts on this question.

1. Are you familiar with your church's statement of purpose? How important do you think it is for churches to have a written purpose? Explain.

_____

_____

_____

BIBLE READING

Read Acts 10:24–35 from the NCV or the NKJV.

NCV

²⁴On the following day they came to Caesarea. Cornelius was waiting for them and had called together his relatives and close friends. ²⁵When Peter entered, Cornelius met him, fell at his feet, and worshiped him. ²⁶But Peter helped him up, saying, "Stand up. I too am only a human." ²⁷As he talked with Cornelius, Peter went inside where he saw many people gathered. ²⁸He said, "You people understand that it

NKJV

²⁴And the following day they entered Caesarea. Now Cornlius was waiting for them, and had called together his relatives and close friends. ²⁵As Peter was coming in, Cornelius met him and fell down at his feet and worshiped him. ²⁶But Peter lifted him up, saying, "Stand up; I myself am also a man." ²⁷And as he talked with him, he went in and found many who had come together. ²⁸Then he said to them,

NCV

is against our Jewish law for Jewish people to associate with or visit anyone who is not Jewish. But God has shown me that I should not call any person 'unholy' or 'unclean.' ²⁹That is why I did not argue when I was asked to come here. Now, please tell me why you sent for me."

³⁰Cornelius said, "Four days ago, I was praying in my house at this same time—three o'clock in the afternoon. Suddenly, there was a man standing before me wearing shining clothes. ³¹He said, 'Cornelius, God has heard your prayer and has seen that you give to the poor and remembers you. ³²So send some men to Joppa and ask Simon Peter to come. Peter is staying in the house of a man, also named Simon, who is a tanner and has a house beside the sea.' ³³So I sent for you immediately, and it was very good of you to come. Now we are all here before God to hear everything the Lord has commanded you to tell us."

³⁴Peter began to speak: "I really understand now that to God every person is the same. ³⁵In every country God accepts anyone who worships him and does what is right.

NKJV

"You know how unlawful it is for a Jewish man to keep company with or go to one of another nation. But God has shown me that I should not call any man common or unclean. ²⁹Therefore I came without objection as soon as I was sent for. I ask, then, for what reason have you sent for me?"

³⁰So Cornelius said, "Four days ago I was fasting until this hour; and at the ninth hour I prayed in my house, and behold, a man stood before me in bright clothing, ³¹and said, 'Cornelius, your prayer has been heard, and your alms are remembered in the sight of God. ³²Send therefore to Joppa and call Simon here, whose surname is Peter. He is lodging in the house of Simon, a tanner, by the sea. When he comes, he will speak to you.' ³³So I sent to you immediately, and you have done well to come. Now therefore, we are all present before God, to hear all the things commanded you by God."

³⁴Then Peter opened his mouth and said: "In truth I perceive that God shows no partiality. ³⁵But in every nation whoever fears Him and works righteousness is accepted by Him.

DISCOVERY

Explore the Bible reading by discussing these questions.

2. How did Cornelius prepare for his meeting with Peter?

_____

_____

_____

3. Why was divine intervention necessary to bring Peter and Cornelius together?

_____

_____

_____

4. What lesson did God teach Peter?

_____

_____

_____

5. What did Cornelius want from Peter?

_____

_____

_____

6. How did Peter's vision change his view of God and others?

_____

_____

_____

INSPIRATION

Here is an uplifting thought from the *Inspirational Study Bible.*

How many pulpit hours have been wasted on preaching the trivial? How many churches have tumbled at the throes of miniscuity? How many leaders have saddled their pet peeves, drawn their swords of bitterness and launched into battle against brethren over issues that are not worth discussing?

So close to the cross but so far from the Christ.

We specialize in "I am right" rallies. We write books about what the other does wrong. We major in finding gossip and become experts in unveiling weaknesses. We split into little huddles and then, God forbid, we split again. . . .

Are our differences that divisive? Are our opinions that obtrusive? Are our walls that wide? Is it *that* impossible to find a common cause?

"May they all be one," Jesus prayed.

One. Not one in groups of two thousand. But one in One. *One* church. *One* faith. *One* Lord. Not Baptist, not Methodist, not Adventist. Just Christian. No denominations. No hierarchies. No traditions. Just Christ.

Too idealistic? Impossible to achieve? I don't think so. Harder things have been done, you know. For example, once upon a tree, a Creator gave his life for his creation. Maybe all we need are a few hearts that are willing to follow suit.

(from *No Wonder They Call Him the Savior* by Max Lucado)

RESPONSE

Use these questions to share more deeply

with each other.

7. What differences divide believers today?

_____

_____

_____

8. What issues do you think Christians should not fight over? What issues are worth discussing?

_____

_____

_____

9. What can we do to build a sense of unity in the church?

_____

_____

_____

PRAYER

Father, your heart must break when you see selfishness, competition, and discord in your church. Help us to take our eyes off ourselves so that we can focus on the common ground we share in you. Father, strengthen your church by filling us with your love.

JOURNALING

Take a few moments to record your personal insights from this lesson.

If I have contributed to any division or discord in my church, what can I do to make things right?

ADDITIONAL QUESTIONS

10. Why is a lack of unity harmful to the church?

_____

_____

_____

11. How can believers remain unified when disagreements arise?

_____

_____

_____

12. How can you help your Christian brothers and sisters focus on the common ground you share?

_____

_____

_____

For more Bible passages about Christian unity, see 2 Chronicles 30:12; Psalm 133:1; John 17:23; Romans 15:5; Ephesians 4:3–13; Philippians 2:1; Colossians 2:2; 3:14.

To complete the book of Acts during this twelve-part study, read Acts 10:1–13:52.

ADDITIONAL THOUGHTS

LESSON NINE

GOD'S GRACE

REFLECTION

Begin your study by sharing thoughts on this question.

1. What is one of your favorite religious traditions? Why?

_____

_____

_____

BIBLE READING

Read Acts 15:1–11 from the NCV or the NKJV.

NCV

¹Then some people came to Antioch from Judea and began teaching the non-Jewish believers: "You cannot be saved if you are not circumcised as Moses taught us." ²Paul and Barnabas were against this teaching and argued with them about it. So the church decided to send Paul, Barnabas, and some others to Jerusalem where they could talk more about this with the apostles and elders.

³The church helped them leave on the trip,

NKJV

¹And certain men came down from Judea and taught the brethren, "Unless you are circumcised according to the custom of Moses, you cannot be saved." ²Therefore, when Paul and Barnabas had no small dissension and dispute with them, they determined that Paul and Barnabas and certain others of them should go up to Jerusalem, to the apostles and elders, about this question.

³So, being sent on their way by the church,

and they went through the countries of Phoenicia and Samaria, telling all about how those who were not Jewish had turned to God. This made all the believers very happy. ⁴When they arrived in Jerusalem, they were welcomed by the apostles, the elders, and the church. Paul, Barnabas, and the others told about everything God had done with them. ⁵But some of the believers who belonged to the Pharisee group came forward and said, "The non-Jewish believers must be circumcised. They must be told to obey the law of Moses."

⁶The apostles and the elders gathered to consider this problem. ⁷After a long debate, Peter stood up and said to them, "Brothers, you know that in the early days God chose me from among you to preach the Good News to those who are not Jewish. They heard the Good News from me, and they believed. ⁸God, who knows the thoughts of everyone, accepted them. He showed this to us by giving them the Holy Spirit, just as he did to us. ⁹To God, those people are not different from us. When they believed, he made their hearts pure. ¹⁰So now why are you testing God by putting a heavy load around the necks of the non-Jewish believers? It is a load that neither we nor our ancestors were able to carry. ¹¹But we believe that we and they too will be saved by the grace of the Lord Jesus."

they passed through Phoenicia and Samaria, describing the conversion of the Gentiles; and they caused great joy to all the brethren. ⁴And when they had come to Jerusalem, they were received by the church and the apostles and the elders; and they reported all things that God had done with them. ⁵But some of the sect of the Pharisees who believed rose up, saying, "It is necessary to circumcise them, and to command them to keep the law of Moses."

⁶Now the apostles and elders came together to consider this matter. ⁷And when there had been much dispute, Peter rose up and said to them: "Men and brethren, you know that a good while ago God chose among us, that by my mouth the Gentiles should hear the word of the gospel and believe. ⁸So God, who knows the heart, acknowledged them by giving them the Holy Spirit, just as He did to us, ⁹and made no distinction between us and them, purifying their hearts by faith. ¹⁰Now therefore, why do you test God by putting a yoke on the neck of the disciples which neither our fathers nor we were able to bear? ¹¹But we believe that through the grace of the Lord Jesus Christ we shall be saved in the same manner as they."

DISCOVERY

Explore the Bible reading by discussing these questions.

2. What controversy arose in this early church?

_____

_____

_____

3. How did the Gentile believers decide to resolve the problem?

_____

_____

_____

4. How did God show his acceptance of the Gentile Christians?

_____

_____

_____

5. Why did Peter accuse some Pharisees of testing God?

_____

_____

_____

6. What final statement did Peter make to the council about salvation?

_____

_____

_____

INSPIRATION

Here is an uplifting thought from the *Inspirational Study Bible.*

The late pastor and Bible scholar Donald Barnhouse perhaps said it best: "Love that goes upward is worship; love that goes outward is affection; love that stoops is grace."

To show grace is to extend favor or kindness to one who doesn't deserve it and can never earn it. Receiving God's acceptance by grace always stands in sharp contrast to earning it on the basis *of* works. Every time the thought of grace appears, there is the idea of its being undeserved. In no way is the recipient getting what he or she deserves. Favor is being extended simply out of the goodness of the heart of the giver. . . .

One more thing should be emphasized about grace: It is absolutely and totally free. You will never be asked to pay it back. You couldn't even if you tried. Most of us have trouble with that thought, because we work for everything we get. The old saying goes, "There ain't no free lunch." But in this case, grace comes to us free and clear, no strings attached. We should not even try to repay it; to do so is insulting. . . .

And now that Christ has come and died and thereby satisfied the Father's demands on sin, all we need to do is claim His grace by accepting the free gift of eternal life. Period. He smiles on us because of His Son's death and resurrection. It's grace, my friend, amazing grace.

(from *The Grace Awakening*
by Charles Swindoll)

RESPONSE

Use these questions to share more deeply with each other.

7. How does the gracious attitude of Paul, Barnabas, and Peter challenge you?

_____

_____

_____

8. What does it mean to extend God's grace to others?

_____

_____

_____

9. Why is it difficult for some people to receive God's acceptance by grace?

_____

_____

_____

PRAYER

Father, forgive us for the times we have insulted you by trying to earn your acceptance. And forgive us for putting heavy burdens on others who want to know you. We know that you save people, not because of what they have done, but because of your amazing grace.

JOURNALING

Take a few moments to record your personal insights from this lesson.

How does this passage deepen my understanding of God's grace? What difference should this make in my daily life?

ADDITIONAL QUESTIONS

10. What traditions or practices have some Christians added to the gospel?

_____

_____

_____

11. How can we determine whether the requirements for faith taught in our churches are established by God or people?

_____

_____

_____

12. How can we guard against expecting more of new Christians than God expects?

_____

_____

_____

For more Bible passages about grace, see John 1:16; Romans 3:23, 24; 2 Corinthians 12:9; Galatians 2:15–21; Ephesians 2:4–9; 2 Thessalonians 2:16, 17; 1 Timothy 1:14; Titus 3:4–7; Hebrews 12:15.

To complete the book of Acts during this twelve-part study, read Acts 14:1–16:40.

ADDITIONAL THOUGHTS

LESSON TEN

PRESENTING THE GOSPEL

REFLECTION

Begin your study by sharing thoughts on this question.

1. What do you think attracts people to Christianity? What turns people away?

_____

_____

_____

BIBLE READING

Read Acts 17:16–31 from the NCV or the NKJV.

NCV

¹⁶While Paul was waiting for Silas and Timothy in Athens, he was troubled because he saw that the city was full of idols. ¹⁷In the synagogue, he talked with the Jews and the Greeks who worshiped God. He also talked every day with people in the marketplace.

¹⁸Some of the Epicurean and Stoic philosophers argued with him, saying, "This man doesn't know what he is talking about. What is he trying to say?" Others said, "He seems to be

NKJV

¹⁶Now while Paul waited for them at Athens, his spirit was provoked within him when he saw that the city was given over to idols. ¹⁷Therefore he reasoned in the synagogue with the Jews and with the Gentile worshipers, and in the marketplace daily with those who happened to be there. ¹⁸Then certain Epicurean and Stoic philosophers encountered him. And some said, "What does this babbler want to say?"

NCV

telling us about some other gods," because Paul was telling them about Jesus and his rising from the dead. [19]They got Paul and took him to a meeting of the Areopagus, where they said, "Please explain to us this new idea you have been teaching. [20]The things you are saying are new to us, and we want to know what this teaching means." [21](All the people of Athens and those from other countries who lived there always used their time to talk about the newest ideas.)

[22]Then Paul stood before the meeting of the Areopagus and said, "People of Athens, I can see you are very religious in all things. [23]As I was going through your city, I saw the objects you worship. I found an altar that had these words written on it: TO A GOD WHO IS NOT KNOWN. You worship a god that you don't know, and this is the God I am telling you about! [24]The God who made the whole world and everything in it is the Lord of the land and the sky. He does not live in temples built by human hands. [25]This God is the One who gives life, breath, and everything else to people. He does not need any help from them; he has everything he needs. [26]God began by making one person, and from him came all the different people who live everywhere in the world. God decided exactly when and where they must live. [27]God wanted them to look for him and perhaps search all around for him and find him, though he is not far from any of us: [28]'We live in him. We walk in him. We are in him.' Some of your own poets have said: 'For we are his children.'" [29]Since we are God's children, you must not think that God is like something that

NKJV

Others said, "He seems to be a proclaimer of foreign gods," because he preached to them Jesus and the resurrection.

[19]And they took him and brought him to the Areopagus, saying, "May we know what this new doctrine is of which you speak? [20]For you are bringing some strange things to our ears. Therefore we want to know what these things mean." [21]For all the Athenians and the foreigners who were there spent their time in nothing else but either to tell or to hear some new thing.

[22]Then Paul stood in the midst of the Areopagus and said, "Men of Athens, I perceive that in all things you are very religious; [23]for as I was passing through and considering the objects of your worship, I even found an altar with this inscription:

TO THE UNKNOWN GOD.

Therefore, the One whom you worship without knowing, Him I proclaim to you: [24]God, who made the world and everything in it, since He is Lord of heaven and earth, does not dwell in temples made with hands. [25]Nor is He worshiped with men's hands, as though He needed anything, since He gives to all life, breath, and all things. [26]And He has made from one blood every nation of men to dwell on all the face of the earth, and has determined their preappointed times and the boundaries of their dwellings, [27]so that they should seek the Lord, in the hope that they might grope for Him and find Him, though He is not far from each one of us; [28]for in Him we live and move and have our being, as also some of your own poets have said, 'For we are also His offspring.' [29]Therefore, since we are the offspring of God, we ought not people imagine or make from gold, silver, or rock. [30]In the past, people did not understand God, and he ignored this. But now, God tells all people in the world to change their hearts and lives. [31]God has set a day that he will judge all the world with fairness, by the man he chose long ago. And God has proved this to everyone by raising that man from the dead!"

to think that the Divine Nature is like gold or silver or stone, something shaped by art and man's devising. [30]Truly, these times of ignorance God overlooked, but now commands all men everywhere to repent, [31]because He has appointed a day on which He will judge the world in righteousness by the Man whom He has ordained. He has given assurance of this to all by raising Him from the dead."

DISCOVERY

Explore the Bible reading by discussing these questions.

2. What motivated Paul to preach the gospel in Athens?

_____

_____

_____

3. Why were the people interested in Paul's message?

_____

_____

_____

4. How did Paul use his knowledge of the culture to present his case to the Council?

_____

_____

_____

5. How did Paul explain that the true God is different from other gods?

_____

_____

_____

6. What has God proven to everyone? How?

_____

_____

_____

INSPIRATION

Here is an uplifting thought from the *Inspirational Study Bible.*

The prevailing world-view denies the existence of absolute truth. So when the Christian message, which is essentially historical and propositional, is proclaimed, modern listeners hear what they interpret as simply one person's preference—another autonomous human choice of lifestyle or belief. . . .

What does this tell us? . . . To evangelize today we must address the human condition at its point of felt need—conscience, guilt, dealing with others, finding a purpose for staying alive. . . .

So we must be familiar enough with the prevailing world-view to look for points of contact and discern points of disagreement.

It is no different then if you or I were talking with a Hindu, for example, about issues of life and religion. We wouldn't assume that he or she was coming from a Judeo-Christian perspective. We would start from the Hindu presuppositions about the world, probe their world-view, find the points of contact and concern, and then begin to challenge or question those presuppositions. Only then could we begin to present our case effectively. . . .

Our handy prepackaged God-talk won't do. Before we tell them what the Bible says, we may have to tell them why they should believe the Bible (there is a great case to be made). And we need a Christian apologetic that doesn't just make the case for us; it must touch the chords within our unbelieving friends and neighbors and begin to alter their view of reality.

(from *The Body*
by Charles Colson)

RESPONSE

Use these questions to share more deeply with each other.

7. What can we copy from Paul's methods when we share our faith with others?

_____

_____

_____

8. What is the danger in changing our approach and presentation to fit our audience?

_____

_____

_____

9. What points should you include while sharing the gospel with non-Christians?

_____

_____

_____

PRAYER

Father, we cannot communicate the truth of the gospel without your help. Take our fears and inadequacies and use them to advance your kingdom. Give us your heart for the lost, your compassion for the hurting, and your wisdom for the troubled. Speak through us to draw people to yourself.

JOURNALING

Take a few moments to record your personal insights from this lesson.

What is keeping me from effectively sharing my testimony with others? How can I begin to eliminate those hindrances?

ADDITIONAL QUESTIONS

10. What happens when Christians assume that everyone has the same perspective and background?

_____

_____

_____

11. List several cultural factors that you think Christians should consider in their evangelistic efforts.

_____

_____

_____

12. What are some ways you can share the gospel with co-workers or friends?

_____

_____

_____

For more Bible passages about witnessing, see Acts 1:8; Romans 1:14–16; 15:15–20; 1 Corinthians 1:17; 9:16–18; 1 Thessalonians 2:4–13; 2 Timothy 4:2–5.

To complete the book of Acts during this twelve-part study, read Acts 17:1–20:16.

ADDITIONAL THOUGHTS

LESSON ELEVEN

FACING PROBLEMS AND PAIN

REFLECTION

Begin your study by sharing thoughts on this question.

1. Think of a time when you have seen someone display joy or courage even through suffering. How do you think that person was able to be joyful or courageous?

_____

_____

_____

BIBLE READING

Read Acts 20:17–31 from the NCV or the NKJV.

NCV

¹⁷Now from Miletus Paul sent to Ephesus and called for the elders of the church. ¹⁸When they came to him, he said, "You know about my life from the first day I came to Asia. You know the way I lived all the time I was with you. ¹⁹The Jews made plans against me, which troubled me very much. But you know I always served the Lord unselfishly, and I often cried. ²⁰You know I preached to you and did not hold back

NKJV

¹⁷From Miletus he sent to Ephesus and called for the elders of the church. ¹⁸And when they had come to him, he said to them: "You know, from the first day that I came to Asia, in what manner I always lived among you, ¹⁹serving the Lord with all humility, with many tears and trials which happened to me by the plotting of the Jews; ²⁰how I kept back nothing that was helpful, but proclaimed it to you, and taught

NCV

anything that would help you. You know that I taught you in public and in your homes. [21]I warned both Jews and Greeks to change their lives and turn to God and believe in our Lord Jesus. [22]But now I must obey the Holy Spirit and go to Jerusalem. I don't know what will happen to me there. [23]I know only that in every city the Holy Spirit tells me that troubles and even jail wait for me. [24]I don't care about my own life. The most important thing is that I complete my mission, the work that the Lord Jesus gave me—to tell people the Good News about God's grace.

[25]"And now, I know that none of you among whom I was preaching the kingdom of God will ever see me again. [26]So today I tell you that if any of you should be lost, I am not responsible, [27]because I have told you everything God wants you to know. [28]Be careful for yourselves and for all the people the Holy Spirit has given to you to care for. You must be like shepherds to the church of God, which he bought with the death of his own son. [29]I know that after I leave, some people will come like wild wolves and try to destroy the flock. [30]Also, some from your own group will rise up and twist the truth and will lead away followers after them. [31]So be careful! Always remember that for three years, day and night, I never stopped warning each of you, and I often cried over you.

NKJV

you publicly and from house to house, [21]testifying to Jews, and also to Greeks, repentance toward God and faith toward our Lord Jesus Christ. [22]And see, now I go bound in the spirit to Jerusalem, not knowing the things that will happen to me there, [23]except that the Holy Spirit testifies in every city, saying that chains and tribulations await me. [24]But none of these things move me; nor do I count my life dear to myself, so that I may finish my race with joy, and the ministry which I received from the Lord Jesus, to testify to the gospel of the grace of God.

[25]And indeed, now I know that you all, among whom I have gone preaching the kingdom of God, will see my face no more. [26]Therefore I testify to you this day that I am innocent of the blood of all men. [27]For I have not shunned to declare to you the whole counsel of God. [28]Therefore take heed to yourselves and to all the flock, among which the Holy Spirit has made you overseers, to shepherd the church of God which He purchased with His own blood. [29]For I know this, that after my departure savage wolves will come in among you, not sparing the flock. [30]Also from among yourselves men will rise up, speaking perverse things, to draw away the disciples after themselves. [31]Therefore watch, and remember that for three years I did not cease to warn everyone night and day with tears.

DISCOVERY

Explore the Bible reading by discussing these questions.

2. Why did Paul ask the church elders to meet him in Miletus?

_____

_____

_____

3. How was Paul tested during his ministry in Asia?

_____

_____

_____

4. How did the Holy Spirit work in Paul's life?

_____

_____

_____

5. What was Paul's attitude toward the hardships he faced?

_____

_____

_____

6. What was Paul's goal in life?

_____

_____

_____

INSPIRATION

Here is an uplifting thought from the *Inspirational Study Bible.*

After I spoke at a women's retreat recently, a darling gal rushed up to me saying, "Oh, Barb, you are just SO LUCKY! You have come through all your trials with so much joy and victory! Now you get to travel all over the country, be dressed up and meet so many famous people and enjoy being a celebrity. You have really got it all together now!"

I laughed and told the lady that I didn't believe there was any such thing as luck for Christians. Luck doesn't come into our lives, but a lot of other things do.

Look at it this way: One family out of 500,000 lost a son in Vietnam . . . we are one of those families. One family out of every 800 has a child killed by a drunk driver . . . we experienced that, too. Statistics say that one family out of every ten will have a homosexual child . . . we know all about that. And recently I became part of another set of statistics, namely that out of every forty women over middle-age, one will develop adult-onset diabetes.

This is something that is brand new in my life. Although it is considered milder than juvenile-onset, it carries with it all the life-threatening complications. . . . I said a lot more, but the main thrust was that I chose to look at what seemed *good* to me rather than to antici-pate all the gruesome complications that can happen at some point. . . . Pain is inevitable for all of us, but that we have an option as to how we react to the pain. It is no fun to suffer; in fact, it can be awful. We are all going to have pain, but *misery is optional.* We can decide how we will react to the pain that inevitably comes to us all.

(from *Stick a Geranium in Your Hat and Be Happy* by Barbara Johnson)

RESPONSE

Use these questions to share more deeply with each other.

7. Why is it important to recognize that pain is inevitable?

_____

_____

_____

8. How do some people make their problems worse?

_____

_____

_____

9. How can the Holy Spirit help us through life's difficulties?

_____

_____

_____

PRAYER

Father, you promised that there would be faith and strength and hope to meet life's problems. Give that strength to those whose anxieties have buried their dreams, whose illnesses have hospitalized their hopes, whose burdens are bigger than their shoulders.

JOURNALING

Take a few moments to record your personal insights from this lesson.

What burdens are weighing me down? How can I release those problems to God?

ADDITIONAL QUESTIONS

10. Why do we try to handle our pain and problems on our own?

_____

_____

_____

11. What lessons has God taught you through the hardships you have endured?

_____

_____

_____

12. How does this passage challenge you to deal with your present problems?

_____

_____

_____

For more Bible passages about facing pain and problems, see Job 33:19–26; Psalm 34:19; Acts 5:41, 42; Romans 5:3, 4; 2 Corinthians 1:4–7; 4:17, 18; 6:4–10; 2 Thessalonians 1:4, 5; James 1:2–4; 1 Peter 1:6, 7; 2:19–21; 4:12–16.

To complete the book of Acts during this twelve-part study, read Acts 20:17–24:23.

ADDITIONAL THOUGHTS

LESSON TWELVE

LIVING YOUR FAITH

REFLECTION

Begin your study by sharing thoughts on this question.

1. Think of a time when you saw someone respond to a difficult situation in a Christ-like manner. How did this resolve the situation?

_____

_____

_____

BIBLE READING

Read Acts 27:13–25 from the NCV or the NKJV.

NCV

¹³When a good wind began to blow from the south, the men on the ship thought, "This is the wind we wanted, and now we have it." So they pulled up the anchor, and we sailed very close to the island of Crete. ¹⁴But then a very strong wind named the "northeaster" came from the island. ¹⁵The ship was caught in it and could not sail against it. So we stopped trying and let the wind carry us. ¹⁶When we went below a small

NKJV

¹³When the south wind blew softly, supposing that they had obtained their desire, putting out to sea, they sailed close by Crete. ¹⁴But not long after, a tempestuous head wind arose, called Euroclydon. ¹⁵So when the ship was caught, and could not head into the wind, we let her drive. ¹⁶And running under the shelter of an island called Clauda, we secured the skiff with difficulty. ¹⁷When they had taken it on

NCV

island named Cauda, we were barely able to bring in the lifeboat. [17]After the men took the lifeboat in, they tied ropes around the ship to hold it together. The men were afraid that the ship would hit the sandbanks of Syrtis, so they lowered the sail and let the wind carry the ship. [18]The next day the storm was blowing us so hard that the men threw out some of the cargo. [19]A day later with their own hands they threw out the ship's equipment. [20]When we could not see the sun or the stars for many days, and the storm was very bad, we lost all hope of being saved.

[21]After the men had gone without food for a long time, Paul stood up before them and said, "Men, you should have listened to me. You should not have sailed from Crete. Then you would not have all this trouble and loss. [22]But now I tell you to cheer up because none of you will die. Only the ship will be lost. [23]Last night an angel came to me from the God I belong to and worship. [24]The angel said, 'Paul, do not be afraid. You must stand before Caesar. And God has promised you that he will save the lives of everyone sailing with you.' [25]So men, have courage. I trust in God that everything will happen as his angel told me.

NKJV

board, they used cables to undergird the ship; and fearing lest they should run aground on the Syrtis Sands, they struck sail and so were driven. [18]And because we were exceedingly tempest-tossed, the next day they lightened the ship. [19]On the third day we threw the ship's tackle overboard with our own hands. [20]Now when neither sun nor stars appeared for many days, and no small tempest beat on us, all hope that we would be saved was finally given up.

[21]But after long abstinence from food, then Paul stood in the midst of them and said, "Men, you should have listened to me, and not have sailed from Crete and incurred this disaster and loss. [22]And now I urge you to take heart, for there will be no loss of life among you, but only of the ship. [23]For there stood by me this night an angel of the God to whom I belong and whom I serve, [24]saying, 'Do not be afraid, Paul; you must be brought before Caesar; and indeed God has granted you all those who sail with you.' [25]Therefore take heart, men, for I believe God that it will be just as it was told me.

DISCOVERY

Explore the Bible reading by discussing these questions.

2. What life-threatening situation did Paul face on his way to Rome?

_____

_____

_____

3. When did the people on board the ship lose hope of surviving?

_____

_____

_____

4. How did Paul demonstrate his faith in God in the midst of a seemingly hopeless situation?

_____

_____

_____

5. Why did Paul reprimand the men on the boat?

_____

_____

_____

6. How did Paul encourage everyone while warning them of the danger ahead?

_____

_____

_____

INSPIRATION

Here is an uplifting thought from the *Inspirational Study Bible*.

Earl Palmer, in a fine little book entitled *The Enormous Exception*, tells the story of a pre-med student at the University of California, Berkeley "who became a Christian after a long journey through doubts and questions." When Palmer asked the young man why he had chosen Jesus Christ, he answered that what had "tipped the scales" in his spiritual journey were the actions of a classmate who happened to be a Christian.

During the previous term the pre-med student had been very ill with the flu and, as a result, had missed ten days of school. "Without any fanfare or complaints," his Christian classmate carefully collected all his class assignments and took time away from his own studies to help him catch up.

The pre-med student told Palmer, "You know, this kind of thing just isn't done. I wanted to know what made this guy act the way he did. I even found myself asking if I could go to church with him."

(from *Simple Faith*
by Charles Swindoll)

RESPONSE

Use these questions to share more deeply with each other.

7. In what ways would you like to be more like Paul? Why?

_____

_____

_____

8. What does it mean to live your faith?

_____

_____

_____

9. How can we ensure that our faith will remain strong when trouble comes?

_____

_____

_____

PRAYER

Without you, Father, we know it is impossible to live righteously. So we ask you to come alongside us and give us the strength to live what we believe. Help us to stand out as beacons of light in this dark world.

JOURNALING

Take a few moments to record your personal insights from this lesson.

How do I usually react when things go wrong in my life? What can I do differently in the future to demonstrate my faith in God?

ADDITIONAL QUESTIONS

10. How does a hypocritical Christian impact others in the church and outside of the church?

_____

_____

_____

11. How can we remind ourselves that people are watching the way we live?

_____

_____

_____

12. What evidence of faith can others see in your life?

_____

_____

_____

For more Bible passages about living your faith, see Galatians 2:20; Colossians 1:10; 1 Thessalonians 4:1–7; 2 Thessalonians 1:11; 1 Timothy 6:11, 12; 2 Timothy 3:14, 15; 4:7; Titus 2:11–14; Hebrews 4:14; James 2:14–24; 1 Peter 5:8, 9.

To complete the book of Acts during this twelve-part study, read Acts 24:24–28:31.

ADDITIONAL THOUGHTS

LEADERS' NOTES

LESSON ONE

Question 5: What does God promise to people who change their hearts in the name of Jesus Christ and receive the forgiveness of sins? Discuss with your group that the Holy Spirit is a person and not a "thing." How does viewing the Holy Spirit in this light deepen your relationship with Jesus?

Question 6: These early New Testament believers spent their time learning, sharing, and praying together. Ask your group members what specific activities we can do today to follow this church model.

LESSON TWO

Question 2: The apostles performed many miracles in the name of Jesus Christ. Ask participants what other examples they can find of the apostles' great works in the book of Acts. Here are some verses you can suggest they look up: Acts 9:3–6; 9:32–35; 9:36–40; 8:39; 12:6–11; 14:8–10; 16:16–18; 19:11,12; 20:9–12.

Question 3: The crippled man leaped for joy, began walking, and praised God in response to being healed. Ask members of your group how they think they would respond if they were healed from a physical ailment or if they witnessed someone who was.

Question 6: Who did Peter attribute this healing to? Explain to your group why it is important to "give credit where credit is due." What dangers could Christians fall into if they accepted the praise God deserves?

LESSON THREE

This Scripture reading speaks of a great miracle that happened in prison and the subsequent boldness the apostles displayed in continuing to preach the gospel, even to the Jewish council.

Question 1: Sometimes fear grips us when God gives us opportunity to share the gospel with others in the workplace, with our unsaved family members, or with friends. And, sometimes, we encounter people who are intimidating and opposing to the Good News. Have the group identify a specific verse in this reading that tells us what we can do when this happens? Another Scripture you may want to share with your group is Proverbs 29:25.

Question 3: Was the high priest's mandate successful? Have a few people read the following verses that tell of God's victory over death and man's futile attempts to keep Jesus in the grave. Read Jeremiah 15:20; Acts 2:31, 32; Romans 8:38,39; 1 Corinthians 15:54–57; 1 John 5:4.

Question 8: God's sanctifying work in his children sometimes causes tremendous emotional, physical, and spiritual pain. But these are the times when we can truly deepen our intimacy with him and gain greater freedom than we've ever known.

LESSON FOUR

Question 3: Have your group members tell of problems they have encountered with other Christians and how they chose to resolve them. What solutions were effective? Which were not? What considerations were made in arriving at those solutions that *were* effective.

Question 4: It is interesting to note that the apostles *collectively* made the decision to appoint seven faithful men to help serve the widows. The Scripture says the whole multitude liked this idea. Perhaps they were pleased because they could see the genuine care and wisdom used in making the decision and because no single person "lorded" over another. They probably recognized that the apostles considered everyone's best interest. God is pleased when the church functions as a body—each member serving the whole.

Question 12: Read aloud the Beatitudes in Matthew 5:3–16. Discuss how the qualities represented here can be applied to interpersonal relationships. When we take the role of a humble servant of Christ, denying our own desires for the betterment of a brother or sister, God's purposes for his kingdom can be accomplished.

LESSON FIVE

Question 7: Look at Revelations 21:1–9, Matthew 10:28, and 1 Corinthians 15:50–53. Understanding these passages can help the Christian face physical death courageously. Why shouldn't we fear death?

Question 8: The Bible is full of faithful people who fervently pursued God and risked their physical lives. Refer to the stories of Jeremiah (Jeremiah 37, 38); Joseph (Genesis 37, 39, 40–45); and the book of Esther. Each of these people were willing to be martyred for their relationship with God. What specific trial did each face?

LESSON SIX

Throughout the Bible, we learn that God speaks to his people in a variety of ways and asks us to do things that we might label strange, foolish, or untimely. But God sees the big picture and so we must trust his voice. Share with your group the tapestry analogy: God has a plan for each person's life, which is like a huge tapestry suspended above us. Because we are human, frail, and earthbound, we can only view the underside of the tapestry, which appears tattered and knotty. The picture on the tapestry often seems unclear to our eyes, but because God has a perspective that is higher than ours, he can see the other side of the tapestry: a beautiful, finished picture, in spite of its flaws and blemishes.

Question 12: Ignoring the Holy Spirit's leading can rob us or others of the many wonderful blessings God wants to give. Consider the results when Moses struck the rock in anger in Numbers 20:10–12, the consequences of Rebecca's and Jacob's deception (Genesis 27), and the Galatians embracing a "different gospel" (Galatians 1:6–9).

LESSON SEVEN

Question 8: Is there anything too difficult for God? Matthew 19:26 says "but God can do all things." You might want to ask two or three people in your group ahead of time to share how they came to know Jesus and how he changed their lives. Not everyone may have a spectacular experience like Saul did, but a changed heart is dramatic *every* time.

Question 11: Think of an experience to share with your group members when you were zealous about something and sure you were right, later to discover you had been deceived. Explain the consequences of your pride. How did it affect your relationship with God and with other people? How did God show mercy toward you? Refer to Genesis 50:20.

LESSON EIGHT

Question 7: If your group has trouble coming up with ideas, ask how doctrine, music, clothes, cultures, race, age, diet, or worship preferences can divide Christians.

Question 10: You may also wish to study 1 Corinthians 12 and 14, which illustrate how the church functions like a body. Other passages you could study include Romans 12:3–8; 14:19; 15:1–6; 2 Corinthians 12:19–20; Galatians 5:22; and Ephesians 4:3–7, 11–16.

LESSON NINE

Question 1: Many people believe they don't follow any traditions. While that could be true, remind the group that traditions aren't always formal rituals. Traditions are often kept in the way we have our personal devotions, church services, and Christmas celebrations.

Question 2: This issue was greater than merely circumcision. Circumcision represented the entire law of Moses. By saying that the people should be circumcised, they were also saying that they should keep the entire ceremonial law of Moses.

LESSON TEN

Question 9: Give the group Bible verses that will help them share the gospel with others: Romans 3:23; 5:8; 6:23; 10:13.

Question 12: Members in your group may never have shared the gospel before. Encourage them to think about how they would respond if someone asked them how to become a Christian.

LESSON ELEVEN

Question 5: Point out that Paul was not a stranger to difficulties. Read 2 Corinthians 11:16–33 for a partial list of Paul's sufferings.

Question 6: Paul also describes his life's goal in Galatians 1:10; Philippians 1:21; 3:14; and 2 Timothy 4:7. Paul was able to keep a joyful attitude because his goal was to please Christ. Remind the group that we can honor Christ by how we choose to respond to our circumstances.

Question 7: Pain is inevitable because of sin. Sin hurts our relationships with God, each other, and our world (Genesis 3:16, 17.) Fortunately, we have the hope of heaven. Christians can look forward to a day when we will have perfect fellowship with God and perfect harmony with each other, while we live in a perfect world (Revelation 21:1–4).

Question 9: For more on the Holy Spirit's ability to help, see John 14:17; Acts 1:8; Romans 8:26, 27; 1 Corinthians 12:4–11; 2 Corinthians 4:6, 7; Galatians 2:20; and Ephesians 6:18.

LESSON TWELVE

Question 7: If the group is having difficulty answering this question, ask it in more direct ways: In what ways would you like to be more like Paul at work? At home? At church? In your neighborhood?

Question 8: Have the group refer to James 2:14–26. Ask: What did James mean when he said, "Faith that does nothing is dead"?

Question 9: The Bible says much about the need to persevere. See Nehemiah 4:6; Matthew 24:13; Mark 13:13; Hebrews 3:6; and 12:1–4. Remind the group that God helps his people endure difficulties: Psalm 46:1 and Psalm 59:16.

ADDITIONAL NOTES

ADDITIONAL NOTES

ADDITIONAL NOTES

ADDITIONAL NOTES

ADDITIONAL NOTES

ADDITIONAL NOTES

ADDITIONAL NOTES

ADDITIONAL NOTES

ACKNOWLEDGMENTS

Colson, Charles. *The Body*, copyright 1992, Word Inc., Dallas, Texas.

Johnson, Barbara. *Stick a Geranium in Your Hat and Be Happy*, copyright 1991, Word Inc., Dallas, Texas.

Lucado, Max. *And the Angels Were Silent*, Questar Publishers, Multnomah Books, copyright 1992 by Max Lucado.

Lucado, Max. *The Applause of Heaven*, copyright 1990, Word Inc., Dallas, Texas.

Lucado, Max. *No Wonder They Call Him the Savior*, Questar Publishers, Multnomah Books, copyright 1986 by Max Lucado.

Lucado, Max. *On the Anvil*, copyright 1985 by Max Lucado. Used by permission of Tyndale House Publishers, Inc. All rights reserved.

Lucado, Max. *Six Hours One Friday*, Questar Publishers, Multnomah Books, copyright 1989 by Max Lucado.

Lucado, Max. *When God Whispers Your Name*, copyright 1994, Word Inc., Dallas, Texas.

Stanley, Charles. *The Wonderful Spirit-Filled Life*, copyright 1992 Thomas Nelson, Nashville, Tennessee.

Swindoll, Charles. *The Grace Awakening*, copyright 1990, Word Inc., Dallas, Texas.

Swindoll, Charles. *Simple Faith*, copyright 1991, Word Inc., Dallas, Texas.

Wright, H. Norman. *How to Get Along with Almost Anyone*, copyright 1989, Word Inc., Dallas, Texas.